ROCKS, MINERALS, AND RESOURCES

Minerals

Adrianna Morganelli

Crabtree Publishing Company

www.crabtreebooks.com

Crabtree Publishing Company
www.crabtreebooks.com

PMB 16A, 350 Fifth Avenue
Suite 3308
New York, NY 10118

612 Welland Avenue
St. Catharines
Ontario, Canada
L2M 5V6

73 Lime Walk
Headington
Oxford 0X3 7AD
United Kingdom

Coordinating editor: Ellen Rodger

Production coordinator: Rosie Gowsell

Scanning technician: Arlene Arch-Wilson

Art director: Rob MacGregor

Design: Samara Parent

Photo research: Allison Napier

Prepress and printing: Worzalla Publishing Company

Indexer: Adrianna Morganelli

Project development: Focus Strategic Communications

Contributor: Jenna Dunlop

Consultants: Dr. Richard Cheel, Earth Sciences Department, Brock University

Photographs: Lester V. Bergman: p.15 (top); Arnold Fisher/ Science Photo Library: p. 7 (bottom); Peter Bowater/Photo Researchers, Inc.: p. 18 (left), p. 24; British Antarctic Survey/Science Photo Library: p. 17; Robert Brook/Science Photo Library: p. 25 (bottom), David Butz: p. 19 (bottom); Christie's Images/Corbis/Magma: p. 26, Roberto De Gugliemo/Science Photo Library: p. 16 (left); Robert Garvey cover: p. 18 (right); Geco UK/Science Photo Library: p. 21 (left); Raymond Gehmen/Corbis: p. 19 (top); Lowell Georgia/Corbis: p. 30; Jeremy Horner: p. 25 (top); Calvin Larsen/ Photo Researchers, Inc.: 22; Susan Leavines/ Photo Researchers, Inc.: p. 31 (right); Novosti/Science Photo Library: p. 23; Samara Parent: p. 11 (bottom); Ken Redding/Corbis Outline/Magma: p. 15 (middle); Royalty-Free/Corbis/Magma: p. 27 (bottom); Jim Selby/Science Photo Library: p. 28 (left); Alan Sirulnikoff/Science Photo Library: p. 10 (right); The Stocktrek Corp./Getty Images: p. 28 (right); Andrew Syred/Photo Researchers, Inc.: p. 29 (top); David Wasserman/Index Stock Imagery: p. 10 (left); Charles D. Winters/Photo Researchers, Inc.: p. 16 (bottom); Conrad Zobel/Corbis: p. 2; Samuel Zschokke/ Science Photo Library: p. 7 (top).

Illustrations: Dan Pressman: p. 8; David Wysotski: p. 3, 4

Cover: Geologists, who study the Earth, use tools such as compasses, picks, and hammers to find mineral bearing rocks and dig the minerals out.

Title page: A rock strewn beach is the perfect place to start a rock and mineral search.

Published by
Crabtree Publishing Company

Copyright © **2004**

Cataloging-in-Publication Data

Morganelli, Adrianna, 1979-
  Minerals / Adrianna Morganelli.
    p. cm. -- (Rocks, minerals, and resources)
  Includes index.
  ISBN 0-7787-1415-2 (rlb) -- ISBN 0-7787-1447-0 (pbk.)
  1. Minerals--Juvenile literature. 2. Rocks--Juvenile literature.
I. Title. II. Series.
    QE432.2.M665 2004
    549--dc22
                                        2004000834
                                        LC

Contents

At our feet

After eating a picnic lunch, two rockhounds spent the day walking on a pebble-strewn beach. At every step interesting rocks and minerals were waiting to be picked up. They scrambled up a sand dune and found a red shimmering carnelian mineral. A perfectly preserved seashell in a quartz conglomerate washed up onto the sand right at their feet. Thousands of years of the Earth's history was ready to be explored, discovered, and identified.

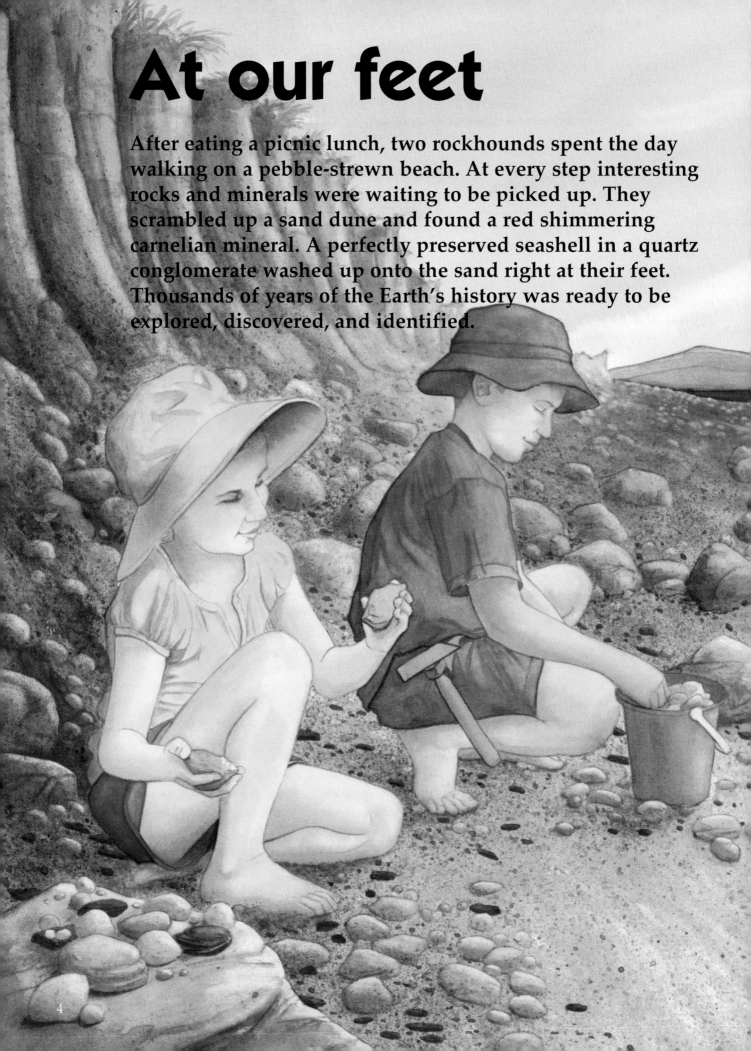

Our Mineral Wealth

All living things on Earth depend on minerals. Minerals are found in rocks and take billions of years to form. Thousands of years ago, people carried mineral gemstones as lucky charms because they believed that they were magical. Gemstones were even ground into powder and added to medicines to prevent and cure common illnesses. Today, minerals are used in the construction of buildings and roads, and in the **manufacturing** of cars, jewelry, and toolmaking.

What is a Mineral?

Minerals are inorganic, or non-living substances that are most often found inside rocks. Some rocks contain many different types of minerals, and other rocks are made up of only one type of mineral.

There are thousands of different kinds of minerals on Earth. Metals, crystals, and gemstones are all minerals that are found in rocks. Silver, gold, and copper are called metals because of their **lustrous** appearance. They are also minerals found in the Earth. Diamonds are gemstones that are difficult to remove from the Earth.

Chemicals

Most minerals are **chemical** substances that are found in the Earth and in the world's oceans. Minerals are also crystals, which means that their **atoms** are arranged in a regular three-dimensional repeating pattern. When minerals are broken, they always form a specific crystal shape.

Chunks of pyrite are imbedded in quartz crystal. Both pyrite and quartz are minerals. Pyrite is often mistaken for gold because of its shiny gold appearance.

(above) Amber is an organic mineral and a gemstone. It formed millions of years ago from tree resin that fossilized.

Mineral elements

Minerals are made up of different substances called **elements**. The mineral halite, also known as rock salt, is made up of the elements sodium and chlorine. Sodium is a bluish-white solid. Chlorine is a greenish-yellow **gas**. When they are joined together, sodium and chlorine create the **compound** sodium chloride. Sodium chloride is the chemical name for salt.

The mineral galena is chemically similar to halite. It is an **ore** that contains both lead and silver. Gypsum is a mineral found in rock. The elements in gypsum make it soft to touch and easy to cut or carve. Gypsum is sometimes called alabaster and is used to make stone ornaments.

Organic minerals

Most minerals are inorganic, meaning that they were formed from materials that were never "living". Some minerals were made from organic, or "once living" material. Organic minerals include coral, pearl, and jet. Millions of years ago, sticky sap, or resin, oozed from trees. Leaves, seeds, and insects became trapped inside the sap. Over time, the sap hardened into an amber fossil deposit.

(below) Galena is a common mineral found in ores that contain lead and silver.

The rock cycle

Rocks are formed over millions of years in a process called the rock cycle. The rock cycle happens when hot melted rock called magma is spewed from deep in the Earth, cools as lava and is dispersed as rock. The lava rock eventually breaks down and transforms into new rock, repeating the process.

Igneous Rock

There are three different types of rocks: igneous, sedimentary, and metamorphic. All rocks are formed through different **geological** processes. The term igneous means "made of fire." Igneous rock forms from hot liquid **magma**. When magma is under pressure, it pushes from the **mantle** to the Earth's rocky outer layer called the crust.

There are two types of igneous rock. Extrusive rocks are formed when magma is pushed all the way to the surface of the Earth. Sometimes the magma cools quickly. When this happens, the minerals in magma form into small crystals. Other times, the magma cools so quickly that crystals do not form. Instead, the rock becomes a volcanic gas. Intrusive rocks are formed when magma cools slowly in the cracks between rocks.

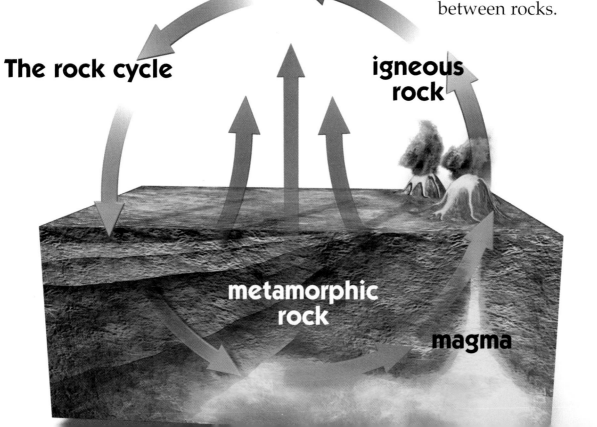

The rock cycle

igneous rock

metamorphic rock

magma

Sedimentary Rock

Sedimentary rocks are made up of sediment, or small rock fragments such as sand, clay, and gravel. Over thousands of years, wind, water, and ice pushed the sediment into lakes and streams. The sediment settled in layers that were pressed together very tightly. The layers then hardened into sedimentary rock.

Metamorphic Rock

Metamorphic rocks are rocks that have changed form. Metamorphic rocks were originally igneous or sedimentary rocks that have gone through a metamorphosis to become a different type of rock. The metamorphosis happened in the Earth's crust where the pressure is very strong and the temperature very high. The pressure and temperature squeezed the igneous or sedimentary rock very tightly, forming a new rock that is stronger, harder, and has a different mineral structure.

(above) The Parthenon is a temple built of solid white marble in Athens, Greece. Sometimes metamorphic rocks have been changed so much that it is difficult for geologists to tell what type of rock it was before. Marble is a hard and massive material that was once a sedimentary rock called limestone. Pure marble is white, but staining produces many beautiful colors.

9

Fossil Find

The Burgess Shale is a rock formation located in the Rocky Mountains in Western Canada. It is one of the world's most important fossil sources and was only discovered in 1909. Shale is a sedimentary rock made up of clay and mud. Fossils of the Burgess Shale were created more than 500 million years ago. Geologists believe that the plants and animals of the shale rocks were buried in an **ancient** underwater **mudslide**. When the mud hardened, the plants and animals eventually fossilized into rock. The fossils preserved the hard skeletal remains of animals that no longer exist such as the five-eyed opabinia, as well as millions of samples of soft shell fossils. The Burgess Shale is a rich source of information on the Earth's history.

Fossils

Many sedimentary rocks contain fossils. Fossils are the remains of ancient plants and animals that have been buried by layers of sediment. Over time, the layers of sediment and strong pressure hardened the plant and animal remains into rock. The remains never decayed and their imprints can be seen in the fossils.

*A fossil of a trilobite, an **extinct** ocean animal. The fossil was found at the Burgess Shale, one of the world's most important sources of fossils.*

Sand

During the rock cycle, rocks are broken down into very small pieces called sand. Sand is made up of exactly the same material as the rocks it came from. Different colored sand comes from different colored rocks. For example, when lava breaks down into sand, the sand is black in color, just like the hardened lava. The pink beaches of Bermuda are made up of pieces of the mineral calcite.

Soil

Soil is made up of broken down rock, plant, and animal life. Minerals from the rocks **fertilize** the soil and help plants to grow. Humans and animals depend on the minerals in the soil for the growth of food. Depending on their geographical location, soils contain different amounts of minerals. The soils of Africa and Australia are red because they contain a metallic mineral called iron.

(above) This black beach in Hawaii is made up of tiny pieces of black lava.

(below) The nutrients, water, and air in the soil allow vegetables, plants, and flowers to grow.

Types of Minerals

Metals, gemstones, and crystals are all minerals that are found in rocks even though they look very different from one another. Minerals can be found in different shapes, sizes, and colors.

Crystals

Crystals are made up of minerals that have melted in the Earth's crust. When the minerals cool, they harden into crystals. Crystals have flat sides called faces. Some crystals grow together in clusters. Other crystals form between the cracks of rocks and grow into separate **geometric** shapes. These crystals can grow to be very large.

(above) A thunder egg is a rock that is the size of a tennis ball. Geologists believe that thunder eggs were formed inside of ancient volcanoes. If a thunder egg is cracked open, a sparkling quartz crystal can be found inside!

(left) A quartz crystal that has grown into geometric shapes.

Metals

Metals are found inside rocks that are called ores. Ores are mined and processed to extract the metal. Gold, silver, copper, and platinum are metals. Some metals are used alone and other metals are combined to form an alloy. Steel is an alloy of iron and **carbon**, and brass is an alloy of copper and zinc.

A karat is a weight used to measure the purity of gold. This dancer wears a 24K gold headdress that is yellow in color and contains more gold than 10K. Jewelry made from 10K gold is not as bright because 10K gold is an alloy, meaning that it contains another metal to make it stronger.

Gemstones

A gemstone is a mineral that has been carefully cut and polished. Gemstones are valued for their beauty and are used in decoration and jewelry. Jewelers cut facets, or flat surfaces, into gemstones so that they sparkle when they reflect light. Precious gemstones are hard minerals that are not easily scratched or damaged. The value of a precious gemstone depends on its color, cut, and **clarity**. Diamonds, emeralds, and rubies are precious gemstones. Semi-precious gemstones are more common and softer than precious gemstones. Semi-precious gemstones include opal, topaz, and aquamarine.

(above) Thousands of years ago, people wore amethyst to protect against nightmares, storms, and thieves.

Identifying Minerals

A mineralogist is a scientist who studies minerals. Mineralogists conduct tests and study a mineral's physical properties to identify and categorize it.

Luster

Every mineral on Earth has its own special characteristics that identify it. The term luster describes the way a mineral reflects light. Metallic minerals are shiny because they reflect light from their surfaces. Minerals that are dull and do not reflect light are called non-metallic.

Copper is a metallic mineral that has a shiny luster.

Cleavage

Cleavage is a term used to describe how a mineral cleaves, or splits, when broken or cut. A mineral that has cleavage breaks along **parallel** lines and fits back together like pieces of a puzzle.

(above) A mineral that has fracture breaks with an uneven surface. Malachite is a mineral that breaks along smooth, curved lines that look like the pattern on a sea shell.

Streak

The term streak describes the color of a mineral's powder. Mineralogists test for streak by scraping a mineral across a tile called porcelain. The color of the powder left on the tile helps to identify the mineral.

Sometimes a mineral and its streak are the same color, and other times they are different colors. Graphite is a gray mineral that leaves a gray streak when scraped across porcelain tile.

Hardness

The hardness of a mineral describes how easily a mineral can be scratched. In the early 1800s, a geologist named Friedrich Mohs invented a scale to measure the hardness of minerals. The scale rates hardness from one to ten based on the softest, talc, rated a one. Diamond is the hardest mineral in the world and is rated a ten.

(top) Talc is a soft mineral that crumbles easily, and is often crushed into a powder called talcum powder. Rock climbers rub chalk and talcum powder on their hands to keep them dry while climbing.

(bottom) Diamonds are the hardest mineral and are rated a ten according to the Mohs scale.

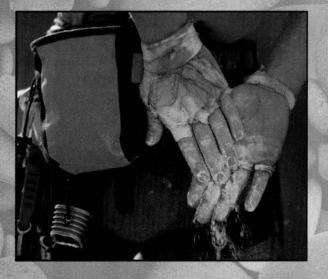

15

Density

Density is measured by comparing the size of a mineral to how much it weighs. Two minerals that are the same size may have different weights. The heavier mineral is denser.

Smell

The smell of a mineral is not strong unless the mineral is heated, struck, or freshly dug up.

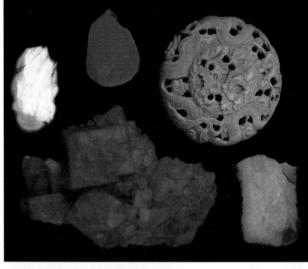

When heated, the mineral barite smells like rotten eggs!

Color

It is difficult to identify a mineral by only studying its color because one type of mineral can be many different colors. For example, the color of mica can be black, brown, or white. Some minerals are always the same color. Cinnabar is always a fiery red color, and azurite is always blue.

A mineral that fluoresces, or glows, when placed under ultraviolet light is called fluorescent.

Lodestone is a magnetic mineral that was used in early compasses to find direction.

Rock collecting

Rockhounds are people who collect rocks, minerals, and sometimes even gemstones. Collecting is a fun hobby that is easy to do and costs little. Some rockhounds collect attractive rocks and minerals to admire their beauty. All serious rockhounds study, identify, and label their collections.

Where to start

Rocks and minerals can be found everywhere. Some of the easiest places to find rocks and minerals are in the backyard, at the beach, and at the park. Other rocks and minerals are more difficult to find because they are hidden under pavement, in the soil, and in river mud. Geologists search for rocks and minerals near mines, quarries, in rockpits, and **outcrops**. Rockhounds can search for rocks in some of the same places, but they must be aware of the dangers and receive permission from property owners.

Equipment

While collecting outdoors, rockhounds should pay attention to their surroundings to stay safe. Some rocks and minerals are found easily because they are already dug up, loose, or broken. Rockhounds wear gloves to protect their hands from the sharp edges of their rocks and minerals.

A sedimentologist is a scientist who categorizes and identifies the origin of sedimentary rock. By studying the layers of rock, a sedimentologist can determine how the rock was formed.

Identify and make notes

After the rock or mineral is found, it can be identified with a **magnifying glass**. The information should be recorded in a notebook. After picking up rocks and minerals, it is important to protect them by wrapping them in newspaper and carrying them in a strong bag.

Hammer away

Geologists, and some advanced rockhounds, use a rock hammer to break off pieces of rocks and minerals from outcrops or boulders. The blunt end of the hammer is used to break rocks. The other end is a pick that geologists use to dig up rocks. They wear goggles to protect their eyes from flying chips of rock while working. If geologists collect by quarries or cliffs, they wear helmets to protect themselves from falling pieces of rock. Amateur rockhounds should be able to find a broken piece of rock near an outcrop.

A geologist examines rock samples in an underground mine in Zimbabwe, South Africa.

Rock Collection

It is difficult to examine a rock or mineral that is dusty or covered in dirt. When rocks and minerals are clean, rockhounds are able to see their shapes and colors. The best place to protect a collection from dust is in a drawer or glass cabinet. Amateur rock collectors can also make their own display boxes out of cardboard or shoe boxes. A good collection has labels that identify each rock specimen, and explain when and where each specimen was found.

(above) Before collecting on private property, it is important to ask permission. Some rocks and fossils should not be taken because they are important to the **ecosystem** *and geologists' research.*

The Rock Tumbler

A rock tumbler is a machine that smoothes and polishes pieces of rough rock. The rocks are placed inside the tumbler with water, sawdust, and **abrasive powder**. When

the tumbler rotates, the rocks are rubbed together, wearing down their sharp edges. The action of the rocks in a tumbler is the same as rocks being tumbled over many years by ocean or lake waves. In a few weeks, the rocks are left rounded with a shiny finish.

Finding minerals

A geologist is a scientist who studies the history and structure of the Earth. Geologists use their knowledge of the Earth to locate rocks and minerals.

For thousands of years, precious metals, ores, and minerals were discovered by luck. For example, the California gold rush began after gold was accidentally discovered in a creek. Over time, the search for precious metals and gemstones became more scientific.

Geographical Surveys

Geomorphology is the study of the Earth's surface. Geomorphology allows geologists to determine what types of rocks and minerals will be found in an area by studying the landscape, soil, and other physical features.

Geologists conduct several surveys, or inspections, of the land to locate mineral deposits beneath the Earth's surface. Some surveys are conducted in the air from planes or helicopters. Special equipment is used to detect minerals that are magnetic and **radioactive**. Ground surveys involve collecting samples of rocks, soil, water, vegetation, and stream sediment. Geologists study these samples to detect the presence of any minerals.

An area that has a lot of rocks made from lava tells geologists that a volcano was once nearby thousands of years ago.

Core Samples

After geologists analyze the survey results, samples of the Earth are taken. Drills are used to cut deep into the Earth and small samples of rock are removed. The rock, or core sample, is analyzed in a laboratory to determine what minerals are inside. Geologists study the core sample to find out how much ore and useful mineral is below the surface, and the shape of the mineral deposit. These factors help to determine whether the mineral can be mined at a profit.

Some of the best known volcanic pipes are in South Africa

Geologists use drills to remove core samples from deep within the Earth.

Finding Diamonds

Earth science has given geologists knowledge of where to search for resources such as diamonds. Diamonds form in volcanoes under enormous pressure and high temperatures. A type of igneous rock called a kimberlite forms from magma inside the Earth's mantle. The kimberlite contains diamonds from deep under the Earth's surface.

Mining Minerals

Miners extract, or remove, minerals from ore. There are two main types of mining: open-pit mining and underground mining. How a mineral is mined depends on how deep the mineral deposit is in the ground.

Ore is a rock that contains valuable metals and other minerals that can be extracted, or removed. The grade of the ore refers to the amount of useful mineral compared to waste mineral. High-grade ore contains a lot of valuable mineral, and low-grade ore is made up of mostly waste mineral. It is very expensive to mine metals. Metals are mined only when there is enough valuable mineral in the ore to pay for the mining process.

The Kennecott's Bingham Canyon is a copper mine in Utah. The mine is the largest man-made hole in the world.

Open-pit mining

Open-pit mining is used when a mineral deposit is located close to the surface of the Earth. Open-pit mining is also called surface mining, or strip mining. Most mineral deposits are covered with layers of unusable soil and rock. In geological terms, these materials are called overburden. Large machines strip or scrape away the layers of overburden to reveal the mineral deposit underneath. After this, miners dig the ore out of the ground with power shovels.

Smelting

Smelting is the process that separates metals and minerals from ore by heating and melting the ore. Smelting is difficult because most metals are combined with other minerals inside of ores. When the ore is mined, drills are used to break the ore into small pieces. At a smelter, the broken ore is heated in a blast furnace at temperatures of more than 2900° Fahrenheit (1600° Celsius). Once the ore is melted, the metal is removed. As the liquid metal cools, it can be molded into many objects.

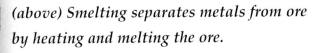

(above) Smelting separates metals from ore by heating and melting the ore.

Underground mining

When a mineral deposit is buried deep in the ground, mining companies must extract the mineral underground in deeply dug mines. Miners dig tunnels, called shafts, into the ground that lead to the mineral deposit. After descending the shafts, they dig out the ore by using hand tools and **hydraulically** powered machinery. Holes are also drilled into the ore and stuffed with explosives to blast the ore into small pieces. The miners are then able to send the shattered pieces of ore up the shaft in rail carts to the surface.

Miners load their trucks with gold in an underground mine in Zimbabwe, Africa.

Aggregates

Aggregate is rock that is mixed with concrete and used for the construction of roads, bridges, and houses. Sand and gravel are the most common aggregates. If they are not available, rock is dug or blasted from a **quarry**. The rock is then crushed, sorted, and shipped to where it will be used.

The aggregate blasted from this stone quarry in Shropshire, England is used for building roads.

Miners working in a gold mine in Choco, Columbia.

A miner's life

Mining is a difficult job. Miners work long hours in cold, cramped conditions and face dangers such as toxins, cave-ins, and poisoned air. Mercury is a metal used in the process of gold mining. Mercury dust blown from open-pit mines pollutes the air, causing respiratory illnesses among miners. The loud noise from drills used to extract rock underground damages the hearing of miners. Miners who work in diamond or gemstone mines must travel through small tunnels in the rock that are deadly if they collapse.

In the past, miners struggled with little pay and dangerous working conditions. **Unions** helped to improve the working lives of miners. Mining companies often discouraged miners from forming unions, because they demanded higher pay. Today, unions are responsible for enforcing the rights of miners, including **pensions** and increased wages.

Uses of Minerals

Hundreds of years ago, painters ground up colorful minerals and mixed them with oil to make paint. Today, people use and depend on minerals for everything from musical instruments to the construction of airplanes and ships.

The Bronze Age

Thousands of years ago, people used tools carved from stone to cut, chop, and hunt for food. During the Bronze Age, a period of time that stretched from 2000 B.C. to 800 B.C., people began to use tools made from bronze. Bronze is an alloy of copper and tin. When people learned how to work with metals, it changed the way that they lived. Bronze axes, spears, daggers, and hammers improved their farming and hunting.

The Iron Age

During the Iron Age, a period of time that stretched from 1200 B.C. to 500 B.C., people began to work with a stronger metal called iron, which they heated and mixed with carbon to create steel. Steel replaced bronze as the material used to make everyday items such as tools and utensils. New weapons such as body armor and shields were also made.

During the Bronze Age, bronze was used to make ornaments, art, and jewelry.

Steel is an alloy of iron and other minerals such as chromium or nickel. Large structures such as bridges and skyscrapers are made from steel because it is a very hard and sturdy metal.

Chalk is made from the mineral limestone.

Building

Metals are used to build houses, cars, and furniture. The concrete, steel, and wiring in buildings are all made from minerals. Concrete is an important material used to construct buildings and roads. It is made from crushed stone, gravel, and sand.

Home

Kitchens are full of metal products and utensils. Refrigerators, stoves, pots, and pans are all made of minerals. Chromium is a mineral used to make stainless steel knives and forks. Aluminum is a special mineral because it is lightweight and does not rust. Aluminum is made from a mineral called bauxite, that is found in some soil. It is used to make cans for soda and food. Sulfur is a mineral that is used to make rubber, which is found in sinks, cooking tools, and in most appliances.

Health and Protection

Minerals are important because they keep people healthy and protected. The mineral kaolin is added to some medicines because it absorbs poisons in the body. Fluoride is a mineral that is often added to city tap water and toothpastes because it protects teeth from cavities.

(above) Asbestos is a mineral that is used for protection from heat or fire. Asbestos is heatproof and fireproof. Firefighters wear suits made of asbestos that protect them from flames and heat while extinguishing fires.

(left) Plaster of paris is a fine white powder that contains the mineral gypsum. The powder is mixed with water, and hardens when it is left to dry. Plaster casts are used to help heal broken bones.

Minerals in technology

Silicon is an element that is very important to humans. Silicon is a bluish-gray solid that can be found in the minerals asbestos, feldspar, and mica. The manufacturing of cellular phones, televisions, radios, and silicon chips for computers are all made from silicon because it is a good conductor of electricity.

The Statue of Liberty is covered with a copper sheet to protect it from rust. Copper is a mineral that is mined and processed for use in making pipes and electrical wiring.

Diamond tools

Gemstones are used to make industrial equipment because they are very hard minerals. In fact, 80 percent of all diamonds that are mined are used for industry and not for jewelry. Low quality diamonds, called bort, are used to make cutting tools such as blades and saws.

(above) Silicon chips like this one are the basis of computer technology.

29

Mineral Pollution

The exploration and mining of minerals sometimes damages the environment by polluting the air, water, and land. Many mining companies try to restore the land to the way that it was before the mining began by developing new processes for extracting minerals and metals from ore.

Tailings ponds

After metals and minerals have been removed from ore, the waste rock, clay, sand, and **toxic** metals that are left over are called the tailings. Mining companies dispose of tailings by storing them in a large dam called a tailings pond. Tailings ponds are found at every mine in the world. If a tailings pond bursts, thousands of gallons of tailings leak into lakes and streams, polluting drinking water, and poisoning fish and animals.

Tailings disaster

On October 16, 2001, a tailings pond burst at a gold mine in Ghana, Africa, spilling thousands of gallons of tailings into the Asuman River. Hundreds of fish, crabs, and birds were poisoned and many people from nearby villages became very ill from drinking the polluted water.

This pond in Ishpeming, Michigan, is red because it is polluted with the tailings from a nearby copper mine.

Roadway damage

Roadways are constructed during the exploration stage of mining so that geologists can travel to and from the work site. In the past, road building was done without concern for the environment and destroyed major **forage areas**, leaving animals without a habitat. Today, mining companies try to protect **endangered** animals by building roadways away from wilderness areas.

Vegetation

Open-pit mining destroys vegetation and trees and leaves huge pits, or holes, in the Earth. Some pits are so large that they can be seen from outer space. In some areas of the world, laws have been passed to force mining companies to restore the land by filling the pits with soil and planting grass and trees. Sometimes the land is turned into farms, and crops are planted.

Building mining roadways in wilderness areas in British Columbia, Canada, has caused caribou to disappear. Many caribou have been hit by vehicles and the roadways have made it easier for hunters to reach them.

Many mining sites are littered with mining equipment, abandoned buildings, and supplies such as fuel drums.

Glossary

abrasive powder A rough powder that wears down rock

ancient Very old

atom The smallest unit of an element. Atoms cannot be seen without a microscope

carbon An element found in all living things

chemical A substance produced by chemistry

clarity The condition of being clear

compound A substance formed from joining two or more elements

ecosystem A community of living things that are connected to one another and their environment

element A substance that cannot be broken down into smaller parts by chemical means

endangered Describing an animal or plant that is at risk of being destroyed

extinct No longer existing in living or active form

fertilize To add nutrients to the soil to make it better for growing plants

forage area An area of grass or plants that animals feed on

gas Neither solid nor liquid

geological Relating to the study of the structure of the Earth

geometric Simple shapes that are formed from straight lines or curves

hydraulically Machinery operated by a fluid, especially water

lustrous Having a shine or glow

magma Hot melted rock formed within the Earth

magnifying glass A lens that enlarges the appearance of objects seen through it

mantle The area between the Earth's core and crust

manufacture To make, especially with machinery

mudslide A slow-moving flow of mud

ore A rock from which a valuable mineral can be mined or extracted

outcrop A piece of rock that sticks out from the soil

parallel Being an equal distance apart everywhere

pension Money that is paid to a worker who has retired from work

quarry A pit from where stone is removed by blasting, cutting, or digging

radioactive Certain chemical elements, such as radium, that give off energy in the form of rays

toxic Poisonous

ultraviolet light Rays, or beams, of energy

union A group of workers formed to protect and promote their interests

Index

1 2 3 4 5 6 7 8 9 0 Printed in the USA 0 9 8 7 6 5 4 3 2 1